MW00884433

# BRITISH CRIME

## True Crime Stories

Roger Harrington

Copyright © 2017.

All rights reserved. No part of this
publication may be reproduced, distributed,
or transmitted in any form or by any means,
including photocopying, recording, or other
electronic or mechanical methods, without
the prior written permission of the publisher,
except in the case of brief quotations
embodied in critical reviews and certain
other noncommercial uses permitted by
copyright law.

This book is intended for informational and
entertainment purposes only. The publisher
limits all liability arising from this work to
the fullest extent of the law.

# Table of Contents

# Introduction

Britain is known the world over for its beautiful scenery, rich culture, and often-romanticized history. As a British resident for the best part of my life, it feels a safe, welcoming place to live, with a soft pull that captures the imagination of people from across the world. But just beneath the surface, something is truly rotten in the state of the United Kingdom, and like most countries, it is no stranger to the evils and horrors of criminal deeds.

Since its formation by the Act of Union in 1707, the United Kingdom of Scotland, England, Wales and Northern Ireland has endured more than its fair share of troubles. From sick child murders and abuse through to terrorist acts, political assassination and some down-right brazen armed robberies, the country has borne witness to some truly horrific crimes.

The purpose of this book is not to glorify or celebrate these crimes in any way. By examining the detail of each case, I hope to shed some light on the circumstances leading up to these events, the plight of the victims who have so tragically suffered life-ending or life-altering consequences as a result, and the mindset of those who have proven themselves capable of committing these heinous crimes.

This is by no means an exhaustive list. However, I've attempted to highlight some of the most significant criminal cases in

British history, to explore the details of some of the crimes that have shaped the British psyche and influenced the response of the British people to criminal threats.

From the crimes of serial killers like Peter Tobin and Harold Shipman, through to tragic child murders like the Jamie Bulger case, this book gives a detailed overview of the people behind these vile acts, and the circumstances that allowed them to commit these crimes before their eventual detention.

For those affected and their families, these crimes have disturbed the natural order of justice, and made it impossible to recover any semblance of a normal life. You will find the details of these cases shocking, but I hope fascinating, as an insight into the mind of the criminal, and the worst excesses of the criminally inclined.

The book is broken into chapters by crime, and I've attempted to group together similar crimes by the classification of their victims. While it is no doubt gripping subject matter, this analysis is dedicated to the memory of all those who have suffered at the hands of these, the worst crimes in UK history, and indeed all victims of crime around the world.

# Political Crimes and Terrorism

**Alexander LItvinenko**

London is a cosmopolitan city, home to around 10 million people across the city and its greater metropolitan area. London has significant pull factors for people from across the UK, and indeed the wider world, drawing millions of visitors each year for tourism and professional reasons. In the last two decades, it has become a center for the global super-rich, with property prices in most parts of central London now far beyond the reach of your average London resident.

A large chunk of the wealth that has come to influence the London property market derives from Russia. The Russian elite have no doubt taken a shine to London, buying up flagship residential and commercial property at a rapidly increasing rate, particularly since 2000. A growing number of Russians now call London home, or at least own second, third or additional properties in the capital.

Aside from being a playground for the Russian super-rich, London is also the diplomatic and political center of the United Kingdom, home to Westminster and the Houses of Parliament, as well as international embassies, envoys and intelligence services.

Alexander Litvinenko had built a new life in London. A former Russian secret agent with the FSB and the KGB, he defected to the sanctuary of the United Kingdom to escape his past, and to avoid the clutches of those who would do him harm. But it was London that was to be the scene of his demise in 2006.

The story of his murder starts back in 1994. Russian oligarch Boris Berezovsky and his bodyguard was being chauffeur driven in a Mercedes 600 when a remotely-controlled bomb was detonated in their vehicle. In the chaos that ensued, the driver was killed, while Berezovsky himself remarkably managed to survive.

Russian agent Alexander Litvinenko was tasked with investigating the crime, which was treated as an attempted assassination. While the details of this crime are not especially pertinent to the Livtinenko case, it served as his introduction to Berezovsky. During the investigation, the two came to know and like each other, striking up a friendship that would endure for a number of years.

In 1998, one Vladimir Putin had risen through the ranks of the FSB, and was head of the Russian security organization. Then a Lieutenant-Colonel in the FSB, Litvinenko was part of a group of dissenters, and having amassed evidence from his investigation and relationship with Berezovsky, accused other high ranking officials of ordering the attempt on Berezovsky's life. While noble in intent, this was to prove a serious misjudgment, and part of the driving force behind Livtinenko's move to the UK to seek shelter from Russian authorities.

In October 2006, having defected from Russian security to MI6, Livtinenko was living and working for the British government in London. Meanwhile, in Moscow, an outspoken Kremlin and Putin critic, journalist Anna Politkovskaya, was found dead in the elevator in her apartment block. Two bullets in the chest, one shot in the shoulder, and a final shot to the head at point blank range finished the job. Investigators noted that the date of her murder, 7 October, was also President Putin's birthday.

Around 10 days later, another former KGB agent had arrived in London. Dmitry Kovtun arranged to meet Alexander Litvinenko at the Itsu sushi bar, where they shared a meal, before subsequently meeting up on a further occasion on the same trip.

By the 19th October, Litvinenko had publicly accused Vladimir Putin of giving orders to kill Anna Politkovskaya, perhaps using information gleaned from these meetings to confirm his suspicions.

After returning to Moscow, Kovtun then flew on to Hamburg, where his ex-wife was living at the time. Subsequent investigations by German police discovered that his ex-wife's flat in Hamburg was contaminated with polonium-210, a highly radioactive substance which would ultimately prove influential in solving the Litvinenko riddle.

On the 1 November, Litvinenko met an Italian security agent in London, who had information about the murder of Politkovskaya. Around 4.15pm that afternoon, Litvinenko headed to the London office of Berezovsky to photocopy the papers he had acquired at his meeting, and to share his findings with Berezovsky, who was now himself interested in investigating alleged Russian state involvement in several high profile assassinations. From there, he set off to the Millennium Hotel, where he was scheduled to reconvene with Kovtun, and with his accomplices Andrei Lugovoy and Vyacheslav Sokolenko.

Later that night Litvinenko started to feel unwell. By two days later, he was in hospital, fighting for his life. On 11 November, Litvinenko made a statement to BBC reporters, claiming that he had been poisoned by the Russian state and was fighting for his life. The British government installed armed guards as he lay in hospital, in fear of further reprisals for expressing this opinion. The Russian government flatly denied these allegations, and continues to this day to refute any suggestion of involvement in any of the murders surrounding this case.

By the 23 November 2006, Litvinenko's condition had further deteriorated, and he was pronounced dead at 9.21pm.

Unusually in this case, Litvinenko was able to tell journalists and investigators of his knowledge of his own murder. The slow, painful nature of his death allowed him to speak out, and to share his version of events to aid the authorities in reaching further conclusions about what had happened.

Toxicology reports post mortem identified that Litvinenko had been poisoned on two occasions with polonium-210, and his body was overrun with substantial quantities of this radioactive material. The substance was also detected at Itsu, the Millennium Hotel, at Litvinenko's home, and crucially, a particular cup from the Pines Bar at the Millennium, almost certainly the cup used to deliver the second, fatal dose.

After Litvinenko's death, Boris Berezovsky confirmed that Litvinenko had suspected Lugovoy as the one who administered the fatal dose. UK investigators sought to extradite Lugovoy to stand trial for the murder in the UK, but were denied by the Kremlin, citing the Russian constitution which prohibits extradition to a foreign state.

While UK authorities remain clear on what happened to Litvinenko, neither Lugovoy nor the Russian authorities have ever admitted to any part in the murder. It became clear after his death that Litvinenko had been working for MI6, receiving a set monthly retainer of £2,000 for his services.

However, a member of the Russian parliament had stern words for Litvinenko, issuing a warning to any future defectors, as well as Berezovsky directly.

"The deserved punishment reached the traitor. I am sure his terrible death will be a warning to all the traitors that in Russia the treason is not to be forgiven. I would recommend to citizen Berezovsky to avoid any food at the commemoration for his crime accomplice Litvinenko".

Lugovoy himself remains at large, unable to stand trial in the UK for his alleged crime. But fanning the flames still further, in 2008 he suggested that he would be prepared to assassinate anyone who stood opposed to the Russian state, in the interests of national security.

The murder of Alexander Litvinenko brings into sharp focus the murky world of the intelligence services. His fate was ultimately a direct result of his work for and against the Kremlin, and while many cite his important contribution to UK security, it remains a tragic end to his life.

While officially Litvinenko's murder has never been tried in court, the UK authorities and those close to him are in no doubt as to the events leading up to his murder. With two separate doses of lethal, radioactive material, which can be directly linked to Lugovoy, Kovtun, and the key settings for their head to head meetings, it looks certain that this was a political assassination, endorsed by Russian security agents, and carried out on British soil.

## Fusilier Lee Rigby

The murder of Fusilier Lee Rigby remains one of the most shocking attacks in British history. Chosen at random, his murder was incredibly barbaric, sending shockwaves throughout the country. An active serviceman, the 25-year old junior solider was off duty on the 22 May 2013. He was walking down the road near his station in Woolwich, London, at the Royal Artillery Barracks in the city's south-east.

As he headed along Wellington Street, Rigby was struck by a car, knocking him to the ground. The occupants of the car got out the vehicle, and using a combination of a meat cleaver and a knife hacked and stabbed Rigby to death. The shocking incident happened in broad daylight, surrounded by passers-by. Indeed, phone videos shot at the scene show people walking by in the immediate aftermath of the attack, completely unaware of the situation that had just unfolded, and the imminent risk to their own safety in being in that location.

Further phone footage shows the attackers, wielding blood-soaked knives as they waited over the body for the police to arrive. The shocking footage left investigators in no doubt as to exactly who was behind the attack and their motives for choosing and killing Fusilier Lee Rigby that day.

After the murder, the attackers dragged Rigby's body into the middle of the road, seemingly in celebration of their atrocity. Their ranting and raving to passers expressed some contrition, but only that women and children were present to witness the crime. They expressed absolutely no remorse for the killing of Lee Rigby, and no recognition for the severity of their crimes.

Those around them continued to film events as they were unfolding, and passers-by were even brave enough to communicate with the attackers and to demand reasons for their despicable actions.

Within nine minutes, armed police were on the scene. Producing a gun for the first time, the attackers threatened and charged police, who were quick to shoot both of the assailants non-fatally so they could be brought into custody.

The attack was committed by two British citizens, Michael Adebolajo and Michael Adebowale, both of Nigerian descent. Two young, local men were responsible for this callous, seemingly random attack, and appeared calm and measured throughout. It is thought that the gun they brought was particularly designed to help respond to the inevitable arrival of armed police, such was the degree of cold-blooded calculation that went in to the planning of this attack.

Their choice of victim was entirely random, and for Rigby, this was a simple case of being in the wrong place at the wrong time. The two men had identified the barracks as the scene of their attack, where they had decided they would find and kill a member of the British armed forces. Rigby happened to be the unlucky victim of their criminal bloodlust.

In February 2014, both men were sentenced for the murder of Lee Rigby. Adebolajo was remanded to prison for a whole life term, ensuring he will never be released for the rest of his life. Adebowale was handed a sentence of a minimum term of 45 years, 20 years beyond the minimum mandatory sentence for murder in the UK.

But what drove these men to commit such a disgusting crime, in broad daylight?

Both Adebolajo and Adebowale were born and brought up in London. Adebolajo was born in Lambeth, and his family was Christians. He had studied for a degree in

Sociology at the University of Greenwich and was, by all accounts, an educated young man with promising career prospects ahead of him. Adebowale was likewise local, and it has been suggested he too studied at the University of Greenwich with Adebolajo. Indeed, his father worked for the Nigerian High Commission in London, while his mother had a career as a probation officer in the city.

Investigators identified Adebolajo as the ring-leader, with Adebowale playing a supporting role. That's not to diminish for a second the culpability of both in the murder of Lee Rigby, but to highly the influence and determination of Adebolajo in particular to commit this crime.

Adebolajo converted from Christianity to Islam in 2003, a move that was to spark a growing interest in radical Islam in particular. In 2006, he had been arrested for public order offences related to a pro-radical Islamic protest, and in 2009 spoke at anti-fascist events organized by the extreme left-wing group Unite Against Fascism. In 2010, he was stopped with a group of others in Kenya, en route to a terrorist training camp organized by the proscribed Al-Shabaab group. After his extradition from Kenya back to the UK, Adebolajo was clearly already on the radar of intelligence services.

During the murder, Adebolajo was filmed speaking to camera. In his explanation, he discussed that the attack was revenge for Western oppression of Muslims, and qualified his choice of victim as a solider, and therefore, in his eyes, fair game for 'retribution'. What is particularly remarkable is the calmness of both the attackers and those surrounding them in the aftermath of the attack. Whereas you might expect running, screaming and shouting, the scene is much more serene than that. In some ways it goes to show the level of disassociation from their actions, and the moral justification they themselves felt for carrying out this unforgivable crime.

Despite feeling like they had legitimate cause, their actions have been rightly reviled by all segments of British society, including high profile Muslim leaders who were quick and thorough in their condemnation of their actions.

While no doubt an act of terrorism, at its heart this case was one of cold-blooded, almost random murder. In particular, the barbarity of the weaponry and the style of the attack separate this from most other murder cases, and cemented its place as one of the most high profile murders in recent British history.

Both men had appeals against their convictions turned down, and remarkably pleaded Not Guilty in court of the crimes charged against them. Despite this, the sentencing judge told the attackers their actions were in fact a betrayal of Islam. Their cowardly murder of an unarmed, innocent man in broad daylight remains among the most reviled crimes in British history, and their names will go down as examples of truly breathtaking ignorance, malice and hate, with disastrous and tragic consequences.

## The Lockerbie Bombing

But while their crime was shocking and a clear betrayal of their values and their community, the Lee Rigby attackers were eclipsed in terms of the sheer scale of devastation by the Lockerbie Bombing in the late 80s. The Lockerbie Bombing remains the most damaging single act of terrorism in British history, which led to 270 people losing their lives over the sleepy Scottish borders town of Lockerbie, 243 of whom were passengers on the flight. There were no survivors on board.

Flight Pan Am 103 flew on the route between Frankfurt and Detroit, with scheduled stop offs in both New York and London. It was a regular passenger route, flying tourist and business travellers across the Atlantic. It was on this outward leg to the USA that a bomb was detonated on the plane, ripping the aircraft to pieces with fatal consequences for the passengers and crew on board. As the plane broke up over Lockerbie, 11 further people were killed as they lay sleeping in their beds, in what has come to be known as the worst terrorist atrocity ever to hit the UK.

It should be noted before we look at the details of the case that the conclusion and resulting conviction for the Lockerbie bombing is highly controversial. Many people close to the case believe that the man ultimately convicted of the bombing, an alleged Libyan intelligence agent Abdelbaset Al-Megrahi, was not responsible for the attack.

Notable critics of the ruling include Dr. Jim Swires, the father of one of the victims of the bombing and a respected medical doctor of decades of good service, and the highly respect academic lawyer Professor Robert Black, who in his own right was largely responsible for arranging the trial of Al-Megrahi under Scots law at a specially convened court in the Hague. Both have been active in campaigns to retry the case for decades. However, this remains far from the mainstream view.

The investigation into the bombing was led by police in Dumfries and Galloway, working in conjunction with the FBI to probe those who were responsible. Dumfries and Galloway is a rural part of Scotland, with a small population spread across a geographically large part of the country. The force was one of the smallest in the UK, so the burden of investigation was overwhelming in terms of capacity, resourcing and investigative experience. Nevertheless, with support from the FBI, they set about gathering the available evidence.

During the course of the investigation, it came to light that there had been two prior alerts warning of a bombing on a passenger plane in the days leading up to the event.

A phone call was made to the US Embassy in Helsinki, Finland some 16 days before the attack, informing them that a Pan Am flight from Frankfurt to the US would be blasted out of the sky. Further, they said that the bomb would be carried by Finnish women unwittingly in her luggage. The call was linked to the Palestinian Abu Nidal faction. While this cannot be linked with the theory of Libyan involvement, it remains an interesting factor in the investigation.

This was backed by a separate warning from the Palestinian Liberation Organisation, who suggested radicals were plotting to blow up an American plane to scupper ongoing negotiations between the two sides.

This was in addition to claims of responsibility from a number of terrorist organizations, including two separate Islamic Groups, an Irish dissident group and someone who claimed Israeli security services were responsible.

These conflicting reports and admissions, coupled with the sheer scale of the crime made this a challenging environment for investigators. A prima facie case was established against Al-Megrahi, reliant to a significant extent on the testimony of Tony Gauci, a shopkeeper from Malta who had recalled selling Al-Megrahi clothing and accessories ultimately found to have been connected with the bombing.

Those who challenge the verdict assert that Gauci was not a credible witness, and lacked the full, detailed recall they would expect from such an influential prosecution witness. In fact, he was said to be unsure whether it was Al-Megrahi who bought the clothing, the exact date of the sale, and a number of other salient details.

The co-accused, Lamin Khalifah Fhimah was able to provide a rock solid alibi, demonstrating that he was in Sweden at the critical time and could therefore not have been involved. Al-Megrahi, who it was alleged was a high ranking operative in the Libyan security apparatus, had no such alibi, and was sentenced to a whole life term for his part in the worst single crime in British history.

Al-Megrahi appealed against his conviction, and this was backed by an enduring denial from the Libyan authorities. Colonel Muammar Gaddafi, the volatile Libyan leader, had always denied involvement, although he eventually agreed to pay compensation to the families of the victims of the bombing in return for a relaxing of economically crippling sanctions imposed on Libya. In spite of the compensation, Gaddafi and his successors still maintain to this day that they were not involved in the bombing.

Officially, the case against Al-Megrahi is closed. He died in 2012, and was granted compassionate release from prison by the Scottish government, a highly controversial decision which was thought to have caused some damage to US-UK relations.

Nevertheless, Al-Megrahi was freed on the grounds that he was terminally ill, and returned to Libya to see out his final days.

Regardless of the debate surrounding his conviction, the fact remains that as the only person ever convicted for involvement in the Lockerbie Bombing, Abdelbaset Al-Megrahi is now remembered as the worst criminal terrorist in British history. Let's hope that's a record that remains in-tact forever.

## David Copeland

David John Copeland was a young, delusional supremacist who would come to be known as the London Nail Bomber. On April 30th 1999, Copeland would carry out multiple racially-motivated attacks on the streets of London which would result in the deaths of three people and injuring many more. The intent of his attacks was targeted towards minority hubs and areas with large ethnic populations.

From a young age, David Copeland had an obsession with acts of sadism and cruelty. By the time he was 12, David reported to have harbored fantasies of being reincarnated as a Nazi officer who would have access to explosives, medical equipment for experimentation, and women to act as his slaves.

By his early twenties, Copeland joined the British National Party in order to find an outlet for his fascist and racist beliefs. It was in the BNP that his mind was molded by the more experienced right-wing and anti-immigration enthusiasts. It was around the same time that Copeland began experimenting with explosives and taught himself the intricate methods of creating homemade bombs.

Copeland's view on political violence did not marry up with the beliefs of the BNP, so Copeland left them in order to join the National Socialist Movement. The ideologies of the NSM - especially in regards to violent attacks - mirrored Copeland's own values. He would eventually become the regional leader of the NSM in the Hampshire area shortly before he carried out his attacks.

April 17th 1999. Copeland had created a nail bomb using firework explosives and left it outside a supermarket in Electric Avenue,

Brixton. At around 5pm that evening, the bomb detonated causing injury to around fifty people.

A week later, Copeland would plant a second explosive on Hanbury Street. The area is largely known for its Asian culture, which were Copeland's primary targets. The bomb detonated on the afternoon of April 24th, injuring thirteen people.

Copeland's final bomb was left inside a pub in Old Compton Street, a hub for London's gay community. It exploded on the evening of April 30th. The compacted area which the bomb detonated in caused horrific, life-altering injuries to a total seventy-nine people, and caused the deaths of three people, one of whom was four months pregnant.

CCTV footage of Copeland's planting his first bomb was released to the public and he was soon identified. He was arrested and immediately confessed to all three attacks.

Inside Copeland's flat, police discovered Nazi flags adorning the walls and newspaper clippings of stories about bomb attacks, in addition to explosive materials, a crossbow, hunting knives and pistols. There was no doubt that Copeland was their culprit.

When questioned about his motives, Copeland claimed that his intention was to start a race war. He wanted to "spread fear, resentment and hatred throughout the country". He thought bombing minorities would make them lash out, which would be the "the spark that would set fire to the country". When asked why this was his intentions, Copeland told police that it was because he believed in a master race.

Copeland was a loner. He was confused about his sexuality and his primary motivation for killing others was homophobia and an ingrained sense of racism. He attempted to reduce his sentence via claims of severe mental illness but his prosecution did not accept his reasons. Copeland was quick to claim that his attacks were not in any way linked to the BNP or NSM, and that everything he done was down to his personal beliefs. Copeland's loneliness made him desire fame and notoriety, which he could only achieve through destruction.

It became clear that Copeland did suffer from a form of mental illness, although what exactly his diagnosis is debated by psychiatrists. Five mental health experts claim that Copeland suffered from a form of paranoid schizophrenia and had done for the majority of his life, but this was disputed by the jury in order to not allow Copeland a reduced sentenced on the grounds of diminished responsibility. Eventually, Copeland was sentenced to six life sentences due to the deaths he had caused the severity of the injuries to many others.

# Crimes Committed By the Young

Arguably some of the most horrific crimes are those involving children and young people, perhaps more so when the criminals are of a similar age. Some of the most graphic crimes in British history have been committed by children and young people, and more often than not their victims themselves have their whole lives ahead of them.

This raises a number of moral questions, and goes to the root of our understanding of good and evil. Are these children inherently bad, is it society's or the parents' fault, or are these horrendous examples of childhood misdeed gone awry? In the cases we're about to cover, those involved most certainly demonstrated evil behavior, and amongst them committed some of the most heinous murders in recent British history.

**Becky Watts Murder**

Becky Watts went missing back in February 2015. A 16-year old schoolgirl from Bristol in England's south-west, her disappearance was a prominent news story in the UK at the time. Significant public search efforts were undertaken, and for a while, Becky Watts' disappearance was at the foremost prominence in the national consciousness. Despite their best efforts and well wishes, Becky's body was found on the 3rd March, within walking distance of her home.

Her dismembered body was key to a horrific, unsettling crime that will be remembered as one of the country's most shocking. Becky Watts lived in the Crown Hill area of Bristol with her dad and her stepmother. On the 18th February, she had been staying overnight locally at a friend's house, returning to her home on the morning of the 19th. She had then presumably left the house afterwards without telling her parents, and was last seen by her stepmother at 11.15am on the morning of the 19th. By that evening, she had been reported missing.

From the 20th to 23rd February, police and press appeals for Becky to come home were reaching the length and breadth of the country, and even gaining international traction on social media.

Meanwhile, investigating officers had been conducting extensive searches of nearby open spaces, and conducting thorough door to door inquiries, in search of any further information about Becky's whereabouts.

By the 28th February, holes in the accounts of some of those closest to the victim were coming to light. Crucial information about Becky leaving home on the morning of the 19th had been provided by her stepbrother, Nathan Matthews and his girlfriend Shauna Hoare, 28 and 21 years old respectively. The glare of suspicion fell upon the stepbrother and his girlfriend. It transpired they had falsely steered the investigation in the direction of a disappearance, to cover the fact they were both at home with Becky at the time of her disappearance.

On the same day, police arrested Matthews and Hoare on suspicion of the murder of Rebecca Watts. The truly shocking realization broke headline news. Police suspected Becky's own stepbrother, working in cohort with his young girlfriend, of being responsible for murdering her, and were investigating her disappearance as a murder.

Three days later, the pair was re-arrested. From initial suspicions, the police went on to find her dismembered body, giving further probable cause to the involvement of Matthews and Hoare. What started as a missing person's case quickly turned into a possible murder case, before being confirmed as the gruesome, brutal murder of a younger sibling.

The prosecution case alleged that Matthews and Hoare were at home with Becky on the morning of the 19th. They suggested that Becky was suffocated after she was kidnapped by her attackers, coming to her death in her own bedroom. After they killed her, they stored her body in the boot of their car for a number of hours, during which time other family members returned to the home. The pair returned to their own home and set about getting rid of the evidence. They hacked and cut up Becky's body into small parts, to be held in boxes that would be stored by a local neighbor on their behalf, who had no known involvement in the crime.

Text messages exchanged between Matthews and Hoare in the months leading up to the murder expressed what prosecutors alleged to be an unhealthy sexual fascination for young teenage girls, with both Matthews and Hoare discussing kidnapping fantasies around girls. Hoare described these as 'unfortunate', in denying any knowledge of or involvement in Becky's death. But this wasn't an argument that resonated with the jury.

DNA evidence linking both Matthews and Hoare to the shed where the body was discovered, along with CCTV showing Matthews buying the saw used to dismember her body and both murderers buying volumes of cleaning products in the days after her death.

At trial, Nathan Matthews was found guilty of the murder of Rebecca Watts, while his girlfriend Shauna Hoare was found guilty of manslaughter, with both also convicted on charges including conspiracy to kidnap, possession of offensive weapons in relation to stun guns used in the kidnap, and preventing lawful burying by dismembering. The Court of Appeal is the highest court to have rejected grounds for an appeal against the convictions in this case, saying there is no suggestion that the court's judgement or sentence was anything other than sound.

The murder of Becky Watts robbed a young, teenage girl of her opportunity at life. For the sexual purposes of her deviant stepbrother and his girlfriend, this case of kidnap, murder and dismemberment absolutely destroyed a family, and cause untold grief to those who knew and loved the victim. The heartless nature of the crime, so selfish and so brutal to someone these murderers should have been protecting, sent shockwaves throughout the country and further afield.

The chilling element of this case is in both the close level of the relationship between Nathan Matthews and his victim, and also the clear involvement of his young girlfriend, based on their shared sexual interest in teenage girls. A sickening case of murder in the family, Matthews and Hoare were sentenced to 33 and 17 years in jail respectively.

## The Murder of Jamie Bulger

Few crimes shock and appall the nation to the extent of the murder of James Patrick Bulger. The body of a two-year-old boy was discovered at a railway line in Walton, Liverpool, some two miles from where he was last seen several days earlier. His injuries were horrific, demonstrating one of the most serious cases of abuse ever witnessed in a case of this kind. To make matters worse, the perpetrators were revealed to be two ten-year-old children.

Robert Thompson and Jon Venables were children themselves when they repeatedly attacked and ultimately murdered a defenseless toddler. The severity of their crime raised key questions about our understanding of inherent evil, and the level of disturbance that would drive two children to commit such an atrocious series of acts against such a vulnerable victim.

The Jamie Bulger case is fascinating in its horror, but it remains the type of case even true crime writers feel truly unsettled exploring. Nevertheless, in its context as one of the most heinous crimes committed in British criminal history, the Jamie Bulger case will remain long studied for its shocking, vile detail.

Young Bulger was led away by these two older children from a local shopping center to secluded railway lines. The two older children repeatedly tortured the body, leaving him with a number of horrific injuries that in their own right could have been fatal. Suffering unimaginable cruelty, Bulger was left to die on the track, intentionally laid there by his attackers, who in so doing exposed a callous intent to kill.

The precise details of the attack point to the sadistic, twisted minds of the perpetrators. The level of violence on display from these criminals far surpasses that which most law enforcement officers encounter throughout their entire careers. Those investigating the case at the time were in fact traumatized by their work, which came as particularly shocking news given the age of those responsible.

When young Jamie Bulger was discovered, his injuries were many. The two-year old had suffered some 42 separate injuries as a result of the attack, including numerous fractures. Twenty-two cuts, bruises and grazes were identified on his face and head, with a further 20 series bruises identified elsewhere on his body. Experts said the injuries were consistent with an iron bar, or a brick, or some other blunt heavy object being used to strike the infant some 30 or more times. These lines up with evidence recovered from the scene, including a blood-soaked stone and an iron bar, near which traces of blood were found.

The child's underpants had been removed in the attack and were found discarded nearby. Injuries to his legs and to the lower half of his body had been inflicted on naked skin, a factor that particularly shocked investigators and points to a possible degree of sexual motive to this vile attack. The victim suffered extensive fracturing to his skull and head, as well as serious brain damage as a result of the attacks. It was thought that he had also been stamped upon and kicked, with other injuries consistent with this kind of attack.

This is by no means an exhaustive list of the injuries this child suffered at the hands of his attackers. Some of the vilest elements of the crime have been deliberately omitted, given the particularly heinous and relatively recent nature of his murder. While the nation mourned for young Jamie, it turned attention to wider concerns - specifically, what could drive two ten year old children to commit such an atrocity?

The first reaction was, understandably, that these two children were 'monsters', psychopathic killers, or just pure evil. Violence and murder would be enough in most cases to attract these labels, but the violence in the Bulger case was seen by many as a new watershed - something truly horrific that shocked Britain to its core.

Some have laid the blame squarely on the parents. The mothers of the two perpetrators were attacked themselves and abused in the street by passersby, reflecting the strength of feeling that arose when details of this case came to light. Interestingly, the boys' fathers were not subject to the same degree of hostility, and have been seemingly absolved of responsibility in the eyes of vigilantes and members of the public.

Some suggested a lack of care or love, or just general failings as parents were justification enough to lay blame at the door of the mothers. This was particularly exacerbated by the fact that the attackers, aged just 10, fell below the legal age for criminal responsibility in British courts. In the absence of anyone who could be deemed morally responsible to blame, much of the early backlash was targeted at the mothers specifically.

While clearly an understandable reaction, and certainly a source for further examination into why these boys behaved the way they did, it is still important to distinguish the mothers from this case. While they no doubt had a duty of care over their children, and a societal responsibility to bring them up not to be violent monsters, there surely comes a point when the actions of the parent's end, and personal responsibility from Thomson and Venables themselves must come into play.

The age of criminal responsibility suggests that legally, neither of the attackers could be deemed to have been criminally responsible for their actions. This was not a popular state of affairs, and led to accusations of these attackers being given an undue easy ride through youth courts, rather than the full legal treatment that would have been administered for adults.

Others have suggested there were wider societal elements at play. The debate as to the motives rages on to this day. Both boys were effectively taken into the care of the justice system, and were given new names and identities to protect them from retribution.

Having been released into society in adult life, unfortunately details of these new identities were leaked through the press and social media. Indeed, Jon Venables has received a number of new identities over the years, after revealing his true identity at several intervals during his life. He has also been found in possession of child pornography, and separately sentences after his release on these and other charges.

As a criminal researcher, this particular case is one that continues to trouble me, and to a much greater extent than many other horrific murders. While all violent crime is shocking, it is the level of the depravity committed by those so young, not to mention the very young age of their victim that puts this on a special tier of vulgarity.

# Gang Crimes

## The Kray Twins

1960, East End London; Seventy years had passed since the horrific crimes of Jack the Ripper and social unrest was beginning to wane. The aftermath of World War II was beginning to subside and London was slowly developing its identity as a cultural capital of the world.

Organized crime, however, was still a very real threat, and it was largely perpetrated by two men: Ronald and Reginald Kray, famously known as the Kray Twins.

Both born in October 1933 only ten minutes apart, Ronald and Reginald Kray were raised on the London streets which would later become their violent playground. The Krays were an old-fashioned London East End family: self-sufficient and entirely devoted to each other.

In their youth, both Kray twins took up amateur boxing due to the inspiration of their grandfather. Soon, the pair made money from their boxing antics, which would be the catalyst to a life of violence. Their childhood disputes with other children and gangs would regularly be settled with fistfights or weapon attacks. They were considered on the street to be the two toughest kids around, and it wasn't long before they had ruins with the law.

Their criminal records would be the reason that their boxing careers ended, and thusly turned to a life of crime to pay their way. By the late 1950s, the Kray twins were running a protection racket out of snooker club they had purchased, and were committing serious offences such as armed robbery and arson. They would use violence and extortion in order to acquire more properties, which allowed them to make their name on the London scene.

By the early 1960s, the Kray twins were seen as celebrities. They were often seen on the London nightclub scene and were regularly photographed with actors, musicians and political figures. Despite this, their love of fighting and brawling never ceased. Both Ronald and Reginald would love to get into scrapes with anyone at any time. Despite their small stature; both standing around five-ten and weighing less than one-hundred and seventy pounds, they were extremely skilled brawlers, and out of the several hundred bar fights and punch-ups they were involved in, they rarely come off second best. Both twins were incredibly tough; strong in upper body strength and accurate in the use of their fists as weapons.

The Krays were able to disguise their criminal activities behind their celebrity status and the legitimate businesses they had obtained. By the mid-1960s they were fully fledged gangsters, with a host of accomplices whom they trusted who the brothers had met on the street or behind bars. They called their gang the Firm.

One particular notable accomplice of the Krays was an East End ganger known as Jack "The Hat" McVitie. Tall, muscular, brooding; he was an ideal candidate for the Krays to employ if they needed someone beating to a pulp. Although they used his skills for beatings and robberies quite regularly, he was never really considered a true member of the Firm by Ronnie and Reggie.

Throughout 1967, McVitie caused a multitude of problems for the Krays. On one occasion, Ronnie paid McVitie a hundred pounds to carry out an assassination but McVitie failed to deliver on his promise. McVitie then refused to pay Ronnie back his money, and when confronted by the Krays, McVitie lashed out and threatened to wreck a club belonging to a friend of the brothers.

Finally, McVitie pulled out a sawn-off shotgun a threatened the owner of another club of whom the owners were associates of the twins. This would be the final straw for brothers, who decided that McVitie had to go – in the only way they knew how.

On an October evening in 1967, the Krays lured McVitie to a basement flat under the ruse of there being a party there. Once inside, McVitie found Ronnie waiting for him. Ronnie immediately began hurling abuse at McVitie and attempted to shoot him in the temple with a semi-automatic pistol.

Ronnie's weapon jammed, however, and instead begun attacking McVitie with a piece of broken glass. This reportedly escalated into a fight. A cousin of the Krays, Ronnie

Hart, grabbed McVitie and held him. Reggie Kray then picked up a carving knife and stabbed McVitie in the face, torso and neck. McVitie instantly fell to the floor, to which Reggie continued to stab at him.

The Krays then attempted to move the body to the premises belonging to a rival gang, hoping they would get the blame for the murder of Jack "The Hat" McVitie. Unfortunately, McVitie's body has never been found to this day.

This was a turning point for the Firm as many of them believed that McVitie's death was entirely undeserved. It prompted them to think that it could possibly happen to them over the most minor of circumstances. Many members of their gang considered testifying to authorities of the Krays criminal activities in order to assure their own safety.

In late 1967, there was enough evidence in the form of witness testimonies for Scotland Yard to arrest the Kray twins. Both brothers, along with fifteen other members of the Firm were taken into custody. Despite their schemes to spread out the murder charges so that their punishments would be minimalized, both twins were sentenced to life imprisonment.

Ronnie Kray died in March 1995 from a heart attack at the age of 61. He remained at Broadmoor Hospital throughout his incarceration. The year before he died, Ronnie published his autobiographical life story under the title My Story.

Reggie Kray was released from prison in August 2000 after serving the recommended thirty years. At the age of 66, Reggie was free again, but was also suffering from terminal bladder cancer. He died less than two months after his release alongside his wife, Roberta, whom he had married while serving his sentence.

Over the years, the story of the Kray twins has become synonymous with the word gangster. Their life stories have been adapted multiple times for film and television and continue to be a cornerstone of British crime stories.

**Hatton Garden Robbery**

In 2015, one of the most audacious robberies in British history was carried out to perfection. The ideal subject for a feature film, the Hatton Garden robbery wreaked havoc on its victims, many of whom lost their life savings in the raid. While the story appeals to a roguish instinct, and is in some respects an impressive feat of criminality, it must be remembered that the gang who carried out this robbery caused extreme anguish and distress amongst those who were unlucky enough to be victims of their heist.

The Hatton Garden Safe Deposit Company was a business operating in London's affluent Hatton Garden district. Famous for its jewelers and high-end retailers, Hatton Garden is traditionally associated with the city's rich, many of whom entrusted the Safe Deposit Company with their priceless artefacts and heirlooms. The Company had a secure underground facility, thought to be impenetrable to outside detection.

The safety deposit boxes were contained in a thick concrete defenses, as well as metal bars, deep in the bowels of the highly secured building. Truly Mission: Impossible style security measures were employed in this place. If anywhere in London was thought to be safe and secure; it was the Hatton Garden Safe Deposit Company.

It was perhaps this level of impenetrability that attracted the gang to plot their crime. Hailed in some quarters as one of the most brazen robbery attempts in the history of British crime, the serious implications of their crimes shouldn't be forgotten.

In 2015, Easter fell in April, with Bank Holiday and Passover happening at the same time, creating an unusually long bank holiday weekend. It was during period that the Hatton Garden Safe Deposit Company was successfully burgled. The burglary was only brought to the attention of the Metropolitan Police on the 7th April. But when CCTV footage was reviewed, it became clear that someone, somehow, had robbed this high security facility some days earlier - on the 2nd April.

This was now a significant criminal investigation, and the Metropolitan Police would need to pull out all the stops to get close to those behind this incredible act of theft.

On the surface, there appeared to be no signs of forced entry into the main entrance of the building. The only method of entry the burglars could have used was to drill through a lift shift which accessed Hatton Garden vault directly.

In order to do this, the robbers would need to misdirect attention from their heist onto somewhere else nearby. Although it is still unconfirmed whether it was caused by the burglars or not, on April 1st 2015, a major fire began below the pavement in Kingsway. It spread quickly, and caused incredible damage to electrical cables and sewage systems beneath London. The fire would continue to spread for the next two days. The sheer force of the pressure built up below ground caused a manhole cover to blow, causing the fire to shoot out onto the Kingsway streets.

The event was so intense it caused cancellations of theatre performances and evacuations of nearby workplaces. It was eventually placed under control by authorities but not without causing severe disruption to the entire area.

The London Fire Brigade would later declare that the fire appeared to have come from an electrical anomaly and there was no evidence to suggest it was created purposely, however, the convenience that the fire occurred just as Britain's most daring robbery was taking place is too much of a coincidence to brush aside.

Police would later reveal footage of the burglary in an attempt to locate the culprits responsible. The video showed six gentlemen whom the press had already assigned nicknames to: Mr. Ginger, Mr. Strong, Mr. Montana, The Gent, The Tall Man and the Old Man.

It appeared that on the 2nd April, just after the Hatton Garden Safe Deposit Company had closed its doors the weekend, 'Mr. Ginger' made his way below ground to access the vault doors. It is believed that for the next several hours, he and his accomplices drilled their way through the door and into the vault.

The gang would not leave the site until almost 11 hours later. It was around 8am on the 3rd April when the robbers vanished with several million pounds' worth of stolen jewelry which they had stored in wheelie bins.

Amazingly, the robbers did not leave it there. Further gang members would return the following evening (April 4th – around 9pm) in order to fleece further goods. They then spent around nine hours there before fleeing.

Just over a month later, nine people would be arrested in connection with the heist.

It appeared the entire heist was masterminded by a previously-convicted burglar by the name of Brian Reader. A further eight men were arrested and were charged with conspiracy to commit burglary and conspiracy to conceal, convert or transfer criminal property.

All guilty party members were uncovered and sentenced appropriately. Each received between one and seven year sentences, with ringleader Brian Reader receiving the longer imprisonment. Since this verdict, many people have claimed the lengths of the sentences are nowhere near the levels they should be; a grand total of 34 years in jail for a crime which robbed millions of pounds.

Unfortunately for the Hatton Garden Safe Deposit Company, the burglary has served to ruin its reputation as a secure location for wealthy people's possessions. On September 1st 2015, a mere five months after the heist, the company announced that it had gone into liquidation due to insolvency.

A grand of 14 million pounds worth of goods was taken during the heist. Some of the jewels have been found – a few of which were discovered in a Sainsbury's bag in a London cemetery – however, there is still a grand total of ten million pounds' worth of items still missing as of the time of writing.

# Prolific and Serial Crimes

## Jimmy Savile

Jimmy Savile was once the darling of the British establishment. Rising to prominence as a DJ and television personality, Jimmy Savile was a positively A-list celebrity and a household name in the UK over at least three decades. His unusual, exuberant image earned him increasingly high profile presenting gigs, including chart music show Top of the Pops and Jim'll Fix It, a show where he made the dreams of young viewers come true.

Building on his celebrity platform, Savile became a prolific fundraiser and campaigner for a number of charities, hospitals and other institutions, earning him some of the highest honors in the United Kingdom - including a knighthood.

He had friends in high places. In particular, Savile was close to Prime Ministers including Margaret Thatcher, as well as a number of other well-respected figures in the British establishment of the time, including politicians from all sides of the house and notable celebrities, businessmen and other figures. Yet there were rumors, decades old, of a predatory streak to Savile's character. Indeed, several documentaries shot in his later life posed some awkward questions about the collective perception of this man, versus the reality. In retrospect, Savile's behavior sees him dropping hints about his past, and about some of the things he might have done. Only with context does it become clear that this man was truly one of the most evil criminals in history.

Unfortunately, it wasn't until after his death in 2011 that Jimmy Savile's true character came to light. The cheeky chappy with an endearing TV personality was revealed to be one of the most vile criminals in British history, leaving at least hundreds of victims who have been abused and worse by this sickening individual.

In September 2012, Savile had been dead for around a year. Some victims started to come forward, claiming they had been subject to horrific sexual abuse by Jimmy Savile. The victims included young male and female children, teenagers, disable and vulnerable people of all ages, and even adults. As more accusations came out, it became clear that Savile was a prolific sex attacker, indiscriminate in his targets and no stranger to the very worst of human capability. Worse, he was using his position of trust and respect to gain access to vulnerable groups of people, whom he would make his victims.

By October, 13 British police forces were investigating separate instances of crimes committed by Jimmy Savile, showing the sheet extent of the allegations across the country. This led to the Metropolitan Police forming a more wide ranging investigation into criminal child sex abuse, specifically focusing on Savile, but extending to cover a number of other celebrity perpetrators and other authority figures at the time. By far the most prolific offender of all those investigated; there remain over 450 separate lines of enquiry against Savile, with the potential for hundreds more yet to come forward. The sheer scale of his crimes is incredible, and the depravity of his actions staggering to even some of the most hardened criminal investigators.

The uncovering of Jimmy Savile's crimes shocked the country, and led to sweeping changes aimed at protecting children and vulnerable people further from abuses like those committed by Savile. As the BBC, the National Health Service and the wider British authorities came to terms with what had been going on throughout their organizations at the hands of Savile, fingers of blame were pointed at other establishment figures who should have reported Savile, or should have been aware of his behavior.

Remarkably, while there were rumors of Jimmy Savile being something of an untrustworthy character, there were few who felt strongly that his was wicked, or a criminal to the extent as has since become clear. In fact, one of his most chilling abilities seems to be his charming personality, which enabled him to become a celebrated cultural figure, and a permanent feature of the British elite during the high tide of his career.

The scale of his crimes is simply unprecedented. As serial criminals go, Jimmy Savile has been one of the worst offenders ever to have been born. Some psychologists have identified narcissistic and even psychopathic traits in Savile's character, which would go some way towards offering explanation for his behavior, and for his choices to abuse and attack innocent people. There are some suggests that Savile's abuse has gone further, spanning into necrophilic assaults and perhaps even murder.

At the time of writing, Operation Yewtree remains active, and the Metropolitan Police are into their fourth year of investigating the crimes committed by Jimmy Savile and others. The case has also resulted in a number of other celebrities being jailed for historic sex crimes, including Gary Glitter, Dave Lee Travis, Max Clifford, and one-time national treasure Rolf Harris. Few would bet against more accusations emerging against

Savile, and indeed against others from around the time.

The picture painted by Operation Yewtree is bleak, and amounts to a culture of sexual abuse, including of children, at the BBC and other establishment organizations in the 60s, 70s and 80s. It remains to this day an unimaginable shame on the British establishment, and amongst one of the worst endemic criminal behaviors to have been uncovered in British history.

Escaping justice only by virtue of his death, Savile never stood trial for any of his crimes, and was certainly never sentenced for any of his wicked acts. This was an evil man who saw himself as above the law, above the call of justice, and died in the knowledge that his crimes were never detected. If only he had been alive to face up to his true evil, and to take the consequences of his crime. It is impossible to imagine any imposable sentence that could be reflective of the severity of his crimes.

**The Soham Murders**

One of the most shocking crimes of recent memory is the double murder of two young and beautiful girls; Holly Wells and Jessica Chapman. The now-infamous picture of the pair sporting big smiles in their Manchester United uniforms still makes the nation's hearts wrench now that the picture has become synonymous with the cowardly actions of one depraved sex offender.

Soham, Cambridgeshire. It was on August 4th 2002 when both Jessica Chapman and Holly Wells, both only ten years of age, left their houses for the final time. The girls were heading to a nearby store to pick up some sweets when they were coaxed into coming into the house of a stranger whom they had passed by. The man was Ian Huntley.

Huntley noticed the pair of girls were walking past his residence when he quickly went out to talk to them. He told them that his girlfriend, Maxine Carr, was also at home despite her not being. Huntley told the girls that Carr was a learning support assistant the same school as Holly and Jessica, so they would have no need to worry.

The girls agreed to go inside Huntley's house. Shortly after, they were murdered.

The same evening, the parents of the girls reported them missing to the police. The parents had no idea what could have happened to them. They simply went to a nearby shop in the early evening and never came back. The ensuing months would be a living hell for the parents of Jessica and Holly.

The police established a city-wide search for the girls with the help of several hundred volunteers. The search would span weeks. Due to tabloid exposure, everyone in Britain recognized the faces of the girls. Their pictures were on the front of every newspaper. Someone somewhere had to know what happened to them.

Many witnesses came forward to claim that they had seen the girls after they had left their home on the same evening. One particularly enthusiastic witness, whose name meant nothing to investigators at this point, was Ian Huntley. Huntley informed the police that the girls had passed by his house around 6pm that day. In an attempt to rule him out as a suspect, police searched Huntley's premises and found no evidence to link him to the girls' disappearances

However, some officers were suspicious of Huntley's behavior. He had injected himself into their investigation with a lot more enthusiasm than all other volunteers which suggested to the police he knew more than he let on. Reports state that Huntley was 'too emotionally invested' in the case for someone who wasn't directly involved, and appeared to ask a lot more questions than was necessary.

A week after a search of Huntley's premises, police made a crucial discovery on the grounds of Soham Village College – Ian Huntley's place of work. The charred remains of Holly and Jessica's Manchester United uniforms – the clothes they were wearing on the day of their disappearances – were found in a garbage bin.

This gruesome discovery, along with Huntley's suspicious behavior, was enough for the police to arrest both Huntley and his girlfriend Maxine Carr. However, Huntley did not immediately confess to any wrongdoings.

It would not be until two weeks after the girls' disappearances that their remains were uncovered by chance. A game warden who was passing through the woods happened across the burnt, decaying bodies of both Holly and Jessica, lying in a ditch behind an air base in Suffolk, around twelve miles from Huntley's residence.

How anyone could bring harm to such innocent children was beyond belief of the general public. Luckily, authorities already had the person they believed was responsible in custody, and the evidence against him was surmounting as the hours went by.

A further search of Huntley's house yielded more evidence in the form of fibers being matched to the girls' clothing. The area where the bodies were found was known to be a particular hotspot of Huntley's, as well as it being close to the house of his father. Additionally, Jessica Chapman had carried a mobile phone with her at the time of her abduction. The last signal which police had located had been in a small clearing near Huntley's home.

Three days after their arrest, Ian Huntley and Maxine Carr were officially charged with the murder of the girls. The pair maintained their innocence throughout and claimed for weeks that they had nothing at all to do with the girls' disappearances.

Over the ensuing weeks, more facts would come to light which were further damning to Huntley's claims of innocence. A witness reported seeing Huntley thoroughly cleaning the inside of his car the day after the girls' disappearances. Huntley is also reported to have removed the lining from his car and replaced all of his tyres despite it not being required. There were also traces of chalk, soil and concrete on the underside of his vehicle, all of which were consistent with the materials found at the site where the girls were disposed of.

Three weeks into Huntley's trial, he would shock investigators by confessing to the murders of Holly Wells and Jessica Chapman. Huntley, however, claimed that their deaths were entirely accidental. He claimed that he was attending to a nosebleed which Holly was suffering from, and in doing so, accidentally knocked her into the bathtub which was full of water. In turn, Jessica then screamed. Huntley attempted to silence Jessica by placing his hand over her mouth, accidentally suffocating her.

Huntley then claimed variations of his original story, all of which were rife with inconsistencies from one tale to the next. It became obvious that Huntley was lying in an attempt to reduce his sentence, but no one bought into any of his stories.

Huntley's past quickly came back to haunt him. Investigations into previous allegations against him were ongoing during his trial. It came to light that Huntley had had ruins with the law on several occasions throughout his life, all of which were relating to sex offences and burglary. However, Huntley had never been convicted of any the previous charges.

In 1995, it was revealed that Huntley engage in sex with a 15-year-old girl. He was 21 at the time. A year later, Huntley was arrested in connection with a home robbery in Grimsby as well as a further incident of underage sex. In 1998, he was arrested on suspicion of raping a woman, although Huntley claimed this was entirely consensual. The same year, Huntley was also investigated on suspicion of indecently assaulting an 11-year-old girl.

Based on the evidence provided and Huntley's dark history of sex offences against minors, he was subsequently found guilty and charged to life imprisonment. During his prison term, Huntley has been a target of violence due to his high profile nature. In 2005 he was scalded with boiling water in Wakefield Prison by a fellow inmate. A year later, he attempted to overdose on antidepressants but was revived by prison staff.

As of 2008 he was moved to Frankland Prison in Durham where he remains to this day.

## Harold Shipman

There is an implied trust between doctor and patient; a trust which is assumed due to the serious nature of the medical profession. Like Jimmy Savile, Dr. Harold Shipman was someone virtually no one would have thought capable of committing any crime, let alone prolifically over a number of decades. A respected GP with decades of good standing, Dr. Harold Shipman was a respected figure in the community, and a much-praised family doctor.

But beneath the surface, behind the professional experience - he was one of the most vile and prolific serial murderers ever to have lived. By the time his crimes were uncovered, he was thought to have killed over 250 known victims, the vast majority elderly women. When he was tried for his crimes, he was in his mid-50s. But evidence now shows he had committed crimes as much as 30 years earlier, and had in fact been abusing his position of trust throughout his career, with fatal results for his patients.

The situations which Harold Shipman fabricated for himself were perfect conditions for a serial killer to operate. For some 30 years, Shipman prolifically murdered his victims across Manchester and Yorkshire, and though he was ultimately found guilty of 15 counts of murder, many more cases have subsequently come to light.

His was the story of the charm of a con-man, a hugely disturbed individual with murderous tendencies who had risen to become a trusted member of the medical community. Working in close contact with patients of all ages in general practice, he was the very definition of a family doctor. He was also a family man who had a loving wife and four children. A family who would stick with him throughout his ordeal, despite the overwhelming evidence of his guilt.

But throughout his career, Dr. Shipman had been deliberately administering fatal doses of the painkiller diamorphine. The flag was raised when a colleague raised the unusually high number of death certificates certified by Dr. Shipman as a cause for investigation, referring the matter on to the police. Unfortunately, the police assigned the investigation to inexperienced detectives, who were unable to find supporting evidence to back up the allegation.

After committing a further three murders, Shipman was finally taken seriously as a potential murderer with the death of an elderly woman, Kathleen Grundy. Suspicion was raised when her will excluded close relatives, to the benefit of Shipman for some £386,000. In addition to the bizarre request, it appeared obvious to relatives that the "will" which Kathleen Grundy had written was clearly a badly-forged imitation. It was carelessly typed and the signature of Grundy did not look genuine.

These initial suspicions led to the confirmation of the high number of deaths signed off by Shipman, which led to further investigations into what had been going on. After a police search of Shipman's offices, they discovered unidentified pieces of jewelry, important medical documents which had seemingly been discarded, and a typewriter which matched the specifics of the one used to type up Kathleen Grundy's fake will and testament.

Once suspicions of Shipman's behavior had been established, a further investigation into his past yielded odd results. It appeared that Shipman regularly told family members to cremate the bodies of their loved ones as a sign of respect, when in actual fact it was a way for Shipman to cover his tracks. Without a body to investigate, police couldn't determine the levels of diamorphine administered.

Despite Shipman's pretentious aura of superiority about being an expert in many facets of life, one area he did not possess adequate skills in was with technology. His claims of being a "computer expert" would eventually come back to haunt him, as it was his forging of medical documentation which would uncover his horrific past. Shipman was not aware that all changes he made to the medical history of his patients were logged on his computer's hard drive with specific details and time stamps. Whenever Shipman took a victim's life via morphine overdose, he would alter his patients' records to give the illusion that they required such an amount.

Shipman protested innocence throughout his trial and never once confessed to any kind of wrongdoing, despite the damning evidence presented before him. Harold Shipman was clearly a serial killer who lived a double life for the majority of his lifespan. Shipman has no discernable motive to speak of, which makes him an interesting case in the realm of serial murder.

Many have considered his motivations to be financial. He did indeed take jewelry and money from a lot of his victims, and the act of forging a will for a significant amount of cash cannot be understated. However, Harold Shipman was a well-paid medical official who was never in debt and did not lead a lavish lifestyle. He never struggled for money throughout his adult life, so it would seem odd that he would go to such lengths for money he didn't need.

Shipman's superiority complex was well-documented by his friends and colleagues throughout his life, so it could be considered that Shipman simply enjoyed playing god and having the power of life and death in his hands.

What Harold Shipman did was create a perfect situation for him to act out his fantasies. He was the trusted medical doctor who was entrusted to nurse people back to health. His patients were elderly, vulnerable women whose deaths would not raise suspicion due to their frail health. They were low risk; they could not physically stand up to him. In many ways, they were the perfect victim.

Due to many of Shipman's victims being cremated and their records being tampered with, it is difficult to determine exactly how many people died because of his compulsion to kill. The common belief is that the number is somewhere around the 260 mark, although different researchers have different conclusions. In January 2004 at HMP Wakefield, Harold Shipman would take his true victim count to the grave. Shipman committed suicide by hanging himself; one final insult to the world.

## Jack the Ripper

The tale of Jack the Ripper has become one of the most infamous in English lore, and by extension British criminal history. Part of the legend and infamy surrounds the fact that the Ripper was never caught and brought to justice. In fact, today, the debate still rages on about his true identity, almost 150 years after the events. His brutal murders in Victorian England have given rise to something of a cottage industry of researchers, academics and authors, who conduct research and publish books to this day with their theories of the true identity of the infamous killer.

There are still various competing theories speaking to his true identity. But what remains clear is that Jack the Ripper is one of the most notorious, brutal murderers ever to have infected the British Isles.

The year was 1888. Whitechapel in London was a poor area of the city, with serious social problems as a result of widespread squalid living conditions. Immigration had become a serious issue across the whole of England, but Whitechapel in particular suffered a significant influx of immigrants, much to the dismay of many of the locals. At the time, race differences were a prominent issue and anyone other than white British citizens was regularly discriminated against.

As well as race and immigration issues, gender discrimination was also prominent. Women were regularly attacked in the street as they were seen as a lesser class. The many attacks on women throughout this time period make it difficult to determine just how many crimes were carried out by Jack the Ripper. In total, five 'canonical' murders were thought to be attributed to him, but many researchers believe he is responsible for more.

Jack the Ripper's first 'officially' recognized victim was a prostitute named Mary Ann Nichols. She was discovered at the side of a road by a in the early hours of an August morning, her body mutilated in ways hardly ever before seen by authorities. Teeth were missing, her body was covered in bruises and she had suffered extreme lacerations along her neck, throat, face and abdomen.

This was only the beginning of Jack the Ripper's reign of terror. From this kill, his intentions only escalated. His following victim, Annie Chapman, a middle aged prostitute, was attacked a similar manner but with more severe lacerations. In addition to the bruises, wounds and deep cuts, Annie Chapman's intestines had been pulled out of her insides and draped across her shoulders in a bizarre theatrical display.

After two officially-linked murders, a profile of the suspect began to emerge. He was thought to perhaps be a surgeon, butcher or medical officer; someone with anatomical knowledge and skilled with medical apparatus.

Throughout history and even to this day, there have been very few occurrences of a serial killer committing two murders in the same day. A compulsion to murder often requires a 'cooling-off period' in order for the offender to reflect on their crimes and to allow their fantasies to evolve. Once their

lust for blood is satisfied, the urge to kill
depletes and then replenishes over time.

Jack the Ripper's third and fourth victims,
Elizabeth Stride and Catherine Eddowes,
were murdered within hours of each other.
Elizabeth Stride was discovered dead
outside a working men's club where she had
been drinking the same evening, although
she had not been mutilated in the same way
as the Ripper's previous victims. Why would
she be linked to the Ripper? If not for the
subsequent murder of Catherine Eddowes,
she perhaps wouldn't be linked at all.

It later became theorized that during his
murder of Elizabeth Stride, Jack the Ripper
was interrupted by a member of staff of the
working men's club, meaning he couldn't

carry out his signature actions (the mutilation of the body). This sent him into a frenzied state as he felt compelled to act out his fantasies that night, and so in turn rushed to find a secondary victim.

Catherine Eddowes would be discovered in a back alleyway having suffered the most brutal attack of any Ripper victim so far. Like Annie Chapman, she had been disemboweled and had her insides put on display. She also suffered severe lacerations to her abdomen, ears, nose, eyelids, shoulders and arms, she had fecal matter smeared across her torso, and the killer had, quite bizarrely, removed one of her kidneys. This fueled further speculation about the killer's profession as a butcher or being part of the medical industry, although nothing would ever come of this speculation.

Jack the Ripper's fifth and final attack would become something of legend due to the inhuman levels of mutilation inflicted upon her. Mary Jane Kelly, a 24-year-old prostitute, was beaten to the point of being unrecognizable on a November morning in 1888. Not only did her murder bear all the hallmarks of Jack the Ripper's previous murders; bruises, deep cuts, abdomen, throat and face lacerations, but she had also had body parts entirely removed. Many of her internal organs had been sliced out and placed next to her body, including her uterus. Her lips had been severed; her neck had been cut so severely she was almost decapitated. Her skin had been sliced so badly that much of her bones were visible. She had been truly pulverized to a point where she did not even look like a human being.

After Jack the Ripper's final murder, he simply vanished. A handful of murders were unofficially attributed to him after the murder of Mary Jane Kelly but they were linked to him tenuously.

Throughout the Ripper's murder spree, many letters claiming to be from the killer himself were received by the police, and three letters in particularly were thought to be genuine. In one notable letter, the kidney which Jack the Ripper had taken from Catherine Eddowes was attached.

Despite this seemingly-concrete proof of the letter being from the genuine perpetrator, like many things in the Ripper case, doubt has since been cast on its authenticity by researchers and investigators. It would seem that since the crimes were carried out so long ago, nothing can really be ascertained as gospel truth. Even accounts of what actually happened vary from witness to witness, meaning that what we know about the case is often second hand information which is prone to biased interpretation.

The list of suspects of those believed to have been Jack the Ripper range from possible (an escaped mental patient with a penchant for sexual sadism) to downright ridiculous (Lewis Carroll). However, these theories simply serve to highlight the prominence of the Jack the Ripper investigation and the impact it has had on Britain, despite the crimes being committed 130 years ago.

We will likely never know the truth regarding Jack the Ripper's identity. The theories and speculations will no doubt continue for the next few hundred years, perhaps getting more absurd with each passing decade. Eventually, like so many elusive villains have before him, Jack the Ripper will become something of myth.

**Peter Sutcliffe**

Peter Sutcliffe, more commonly known as the Yorkshire Ripper, was a high profile serial murderer who operated between the years of 1975 and 1981.

Over the course of 6 years, Peter Sutcliffe murdered at least 13 women and attacked at least ten more. His primary hunting ground was the north of England, namely in the Bradford and Leeds areas. However, Sutcliffe carried out additional attacks in the Manchester and Huddersfield areas.

Sutcliffe was, on the surface, a hardworking man with a wife he loved dearly and who he had been with since his early twenties. He had only ever been with one woman his whole life; however, Peter Sutcliffe harbored a particular fascination with prostitutes. Throughout his late teenage years, Sutcliffe's friends reported that he would constantly bring up prostitutes in conversation, and once also admitted to spying on them from afar.

His first attack would come at the age of 23. On an October evening in 1975, Peter Sutcliffe picked up a prostitute named Wilma McCann from a pub in Leeds. He drove them out to a secluded area under the pretense of using her services, but Sutcliffe waited until McCann's back was turned and delivered a vicious blow to her head with a hammer he kept concealed in his car.

From this point, Sutcliffe would then do two things. Firstly, he would make sure his victim was suitably disoriented (or in some cases, the blows would kill them directly) by hitting them again. Secondly, he would use a knife or similar tool to inflict cuts and wounds into his victims' bodies. The cuts and stabbing wounds he inflicted would be the main cause of death.

For the next five years, Sutcliffe would carry out a further twelve of these attacks, all with the same or very similar modus operandi. He would approach prostitutes at red-light areas in the north of England, take them to a secluded area and attack them when they were unsuspecting. Although Sutcliffe was responsible for thirteen total deaths, his actual attack count was a lot higher. However, his disorganization and impulsive actions allowed many of his targets to escape.

Because Sutcliffe did not plan out many of his attacks beforehand, he was simply left to choose from random women whom he stumbled across during the evenings and early hours of the morning. Because of this, and because he occasionally operated in areas he wasn't familiar with, Sutcliffe left a lot of his circumstances to chance. For example, a large majority of his attacks were heard by passers-by and neighbors, and sometimes even interrupted by people hearing the cries of his victims. This meant Sutcliffe had to flee his crime scenes quickly, occasionally leaving his victim in a state of disarray, but ultimately alive.

The reason Sutcliffe was able to kill for so long, despite being highly disorganized in his methodology, was due to a perfect storm of circumstances. Firstly, Peter Sutcliffe only killed people he deemed to be prostitutes (he killed several non-prostitutes, although he wasn't aware at the time). Sex workers are a very 'low-risk' victim choice due to them being willing to accompany strangers to secluded locations and the general opinion of them being unimportant. Therefore, police may have been willing to turn a blind eye to such events.

Secondly, luck was greatly on Sutcliffe's side throughout his entire murder spree. The West Yorkshire Police were ill-prepared for such a high scale investigation. Their methods of work did not translate well to hunting down a serial killing sexual sadist who was able to hide in plain sight. Due to the sheer amount of evidence, claims, hoaxes, interviews and documentation required, many pieces of vital information were lost in during the proceedings, meaning they were unable to connect vital clues in order to conclude the identity of the Yorkshire Ripper.

Despite their amateurish methods, Peter Sutcliffe was interviewed by police multiple times on suspicion of being the Yorkshire Ripper. However, each time he evaded capture with relative ease. The reasons for their suspicions related to the tyre tracks found at multiple crime scenes which matched Sutcliffe's car type, however Sutcliffe had luckily recently changed all of his tyres. He was also interviewed regarding his number plate being regularly detected by cameras in red-light areas, to which he simply claimed that he had been travelling through them for work purposes.

In a spectacular bout of luck, Sutcliffe was apprehended by West Yorkshire Police on 2nd January, 1981.

At the time of his arrest, police officers had no idea that they had just captured the Yorkshire Ripper. Instead, Sutcliffe was taken in for soliciting prostitutes and for having a fake license plate on his vehicle.

Members of the Yorkshire Ripper Task Force noticed that the man they had in custody emitted the physical characteristics of their suspect. Bushy beard, a gap in his teeth, lorry driver by profession, dark hair, size 7-8 shoe. While he remained under their watchful eye, authorities quickly scrambled to investigate Peter Sutcliffe's whereabouts on the nights of each murder.

Sutcliffe was questioned by police for two days before he confessed to being the Yorkshire Ripper.

Sutcliffe showed no emotion for what he had done during his confession. He described all of his attacks in great, including names, locations and murder weapons used. It would appear, on the surface at least, that Sutcliffe was relieved to have finally been caught.

Sutcliffe was found guilty of thirteen counts of murder and was transferred to HMP Parkhurst. After three years, he was then taken to Broadmoor Hospital due to him being diagnosed with paranoid schizophrenia.

Whilst incarcerated, Sutcliffe has been the subject of multiple attacks due to his high profile nature. In 1996 he was strangled by another inmate. A year later, he was attacked with a pen, causing him to entirely lose vision in his left eye. Again in 2007, Sutcliffe was attacked again with cutlery by a fellow inmate.

Peter Sutcliffe is one of the few living criminals in Britain who are to be jailed for the duration of their life. Despite multiple appeals, Sutcliffe will never be released for as long as he lives. In 2016, Sutcliffe was declared no longer mentally ill by hospital psychiatrists, and so was transferred to HMP Frankland in Durham where he will likely remain until death.

# Conclusion

With a long, rich history, the United Kingdom has unfortunately endured more than its fair share of violence, criminality and cold-blooded murder. From terrorist acts and crimes committed with a political motivation, through to the tragedies of individual cases, the country cannot escape the ghosts of these violent, unnecessary actions.

Fortunately, the justice system in Great Britain is robust, and in most of these cases, the perpetrators have been brought to justice. Some are even still in prison for their crimes today, while others have entered the national folklore for their evil deeds of long ago. Regardless, it is crucial to remember the damage these people have caused, both to the individuals and their friends and families, but also to the wider communities affected by these crimes.

While it is fascinating to uncover the details of these crimes, in an attempt to understand the factors contributing to these callous displays of pure evil, it is important never to forget the victims, nor to unduly glamourize or recognize these crimes as anything more than they deserve.

With every incident, lessons are learned by the authorities, prosecutors and criminologists more broadly. While they can help guide responses to similar crimes in future, unfortunately they can do little to deter these crimes from happening again.

While effective planning and investigation can help deliver justice, these tools are of limited scope when it comes to preventing the essence of evil from rearing its head in future.